BUSES AND TRAMS AROUND LEEDS

JOHN LAW

AMBERLEY

First published 2024

Amberley Publishing
The Hill, Stroud
Gloucestershire, GL5 4EP

www.amberley-books.com

ISBN 978 1 3981 1843 0 (print)
ISBN 978 1 3981 1844 7 (ebook)

British Library Cataloguing in Publication Data.
A catalogue record for this book is available from the British Library.

Origination by Amberley Publishing.
Printed in the UK.

Introduction

The Yorkshire city of Leeds was a little-known place until the seventeenth century, when it became a centre for the wool trade. The Industrial Revolution was the making of today's important city.

This book covers the city of Leeds and those outer locations that could once be reached by Leeds City Transport tram, trolleybus and omnibus services.

The history of affordable public transport in Leeds began in 1871, when horses started pulling trams around the city. Steam-hauled trams were introduced for a short period, but did not find much success. Some electrification occurred in 1890. Leeds Corporation purchased the network in 1893 and further electrification followed soon afterwards. The system expanded and reached out as far as Guiseley and Morley, also connecting up with the Bradford and West Riding systems. The latter had running powers right into central Leeds. Because of the difference in gauge, through running from Leeds to Bradford proved difficult and did not last long.

Closure of the tram system began as early as 1932, with the withdrawal of the Rothwell (and Wakefield) service and more routes were converted to motorbuses in 1934. The outbreak of war resulted in the postponement of some planned closures, which resumed in 1946. Trams in Leeds finally ceased operations in November 1959.

Leeds was also an early pioneer of trolleybuses, with a route to Farnley Moor Top opening in 1911. Two further routes later opened, as feeders to the tram system, bringing Leeds City Tramways into Otley and Burley-in-Wharfedale. Unlike nearby Bradford, the Leeds trolleybuses ceased running quite early, giving way to motorbuses in 1928. Since that year, motorbuses have served the city's streets and suburbs.

Leeds City Transport continued to run a large bus fleet until becoming part of West Yorkshire PTE in 1974. Privatisation saw most of the services transferred to First Bus, the dominant operator in the city today.

Leeds has long been a magnet for other bus companies. One of the largest was the West Yorkshire Road Car Company, which had a fleet that consisted mainly of Bristol/ECW types in the 1960s, due to its ownership by the British Transport Commission. The business later passed into the National Bus Company and was split up prior to privatisation. Part went into Yorkshire Rider ownership, while the remainder was sold to the Blazefield Group and is now in the hands of Transdev. West Yorkshire Road Car also took over the large independent Samuel Ledgard.

Services towards Wakefield were operated by the West Riding Automobile Company (originally a tram system), while British Electric Traction subsidiaries Yorkshire Traction and Yorkshire Woollen District ran towards Barnsley, Dewsbury and Huddersfield.

Wallace Arnold was a large coaching concern based in Leeds. It also ran a few local bus routes under the names of Kippax & District and Farsley Omnibus. Other notable independents included South Yorkshire Road Transport, Black Prince, Rhodes Coaches and several smaller businesses, most of which have ceased trading.

Over the years, the Leeds area has been a very varied and interesting place for any transport enthusiast and the signs are that it will continue to be the case in the years to come.

Looking to the future, is it too much to hope that trams will return to the streets of Leeds? It is reported that the city is the largest in Europe without any form of light rail system. Certainly more electric buses will appear on the roads, but it is unlikely that a proposed trolleybus network in Leeds will ever come to fruition.

The author is grateful to the following for granting permission to use their photographs: Online Transport Archive, Richard Huggins, Richard Simons and Andrew Stopford.

Even in the early days of public transport in Leeds the hub of the network was Briggate, in the city centre. Here, a single-deck horse-drawn tram is ready for departure, as a horse bus stands awaiting customers. Today this thoroughfare is a pedestrianised zone.

Electric trams began operating in Leeds in 1890 and the system soon expanded to cover most of the city. This is an early view, taken *c.* 1900, of double-deck car 34 passing along Boar Lane, heading for Chapeltown via City Square.

In this postcard view, out in the western suburb of Kirkstall, early Leeds car No. 14 negotiates a tight turn exiting Commercial Road.

A later photograph in Lower Briggate and upper-deck passengers have now received shelter from the elements. Car 47, on the left, is heading north for Harehills Road and is about to pass No. 74 on the service to Beeston.

On 20 June 1911, the first trolleybus, No. 503, is ready to depart from Thirsk Row, near City Square in central Leeds, with the inaugural service to Farnley. Built by the Railless Electric Traction Company, this vehicle could carry twenty-eight passengers.

One of the original trolleybuses in the Leeds fleet is seen at its outer terminus beside the Woodcock Inn at Farnley, with its crew posing for the camera, as the passengers sit awaiting departure for the city. There is still a Woodcock Inn in Farnley, but it is a much more modern building.

Leeds trams reached the town of Guiseley in June 1909 and here is a postcard view of the terminus taken soon after. Car No. 27 is ready to return to the city centre.

Guiseley became something of a transport hub after the opening of the tramway, with Leeds City Transport trolleybuses running onwards towards Otley and Burley-in-Wharfedale. One of these can be seen peeking around the corner, dating the picture to after 1915 when trolleybuses commenced. In the centre of the photograph is a Leyland bus, owned by an unknown operator, registered B-8539 and operating a Bradford to Otley route.

Leeds City Transport maintained a depot, shared with the trams, for its trolleybuses in Guiseley and is seen here in 1923. Behind the assembled staff is AEC car No. 514 (NW 2755). The depot still stands today, although it is no longer in use as a depot.

A lovely period view of Boroughgate in Otley and coming towards the photographer is Leeds trolleybus No. 515 (NW 7390). Built in 1924, the chassis came from AEC, while Leeds City Transport built the body in its own workshops.

An official photo of the three double-deck trolleybuses in the Leeds City Transport fleet. Furthest from the camera is No. 510, delivered in 1921, while the other two (511 and 512) had arrived by 1923. Each chassis was built by Trackless Cars Ltd and LCT supplied the bodies.

Leeds City Transport also used motorbuses to provide onward connections from the outer tramway termini. An early Daimler double-decker, registered U-2380, is seen in Shadwell, waiting to depart for Moortown.

A view of the tramway junction in Briggate in December 1911, at the intersection of Boar Lane, looking north. Car 205 is nearest to the camera.

A lovely 1930s view of a busy New Market Street in central Leeds, with trams 298 and 288. The unusual three-track layout here is clearly seen. Note the sandwich-board man in the left corner advertising a sale in one of the stores.

Leeds tram 290 passes the Pavilion Picture House in Stanningley, while en route to its outer terminus at Pudsey. Interchange with the Bradford tram system could be made close to this point.

On 4 May 1920 there was a busy scene in Boar Lane, in the centre of the city. On the left is Leeds car No. 298, while passing in the opposite direction is West Riding tram 35, having just started its journey back to Wakefield. (Photograph by SL Smith, courtesy of Online Transport Archive)

A photograph that illustrates the problems that trams can pose! One of the 1931 batch of trams known as the Horsfields, car No. 174 is seen at Roundhay Park in the 1950s.

Another Horsfield car, No. 177, photographed towards the closure of the system, at Cross Gates terminus.

A second view of Horsfield car No. 177, as one of the ex-London Transport Feltham cars follows along Kirkgate, with the railway and the parish church in the background. Only inbound trams used this section of track.

With the abandonment of the London tram system, many of the Feltham cars, each with a capacity of seventy seated passengers, were sold for further use on the Leeds system. Despite being built in 1931, they were in regular use until the closure in 1959. Approaching Cross Gates terminus, not long before that date, is car No. 528, with its blind already set for its return working to the city centre.

One of the unusual features of the Leeds tram system was the line that ventured away from the city streets and passed through Middleton Woods on its own right of way. Originally served by service 12 (City Centre to Middleton Lingwell Road), cars heading back into the city after 1956 displayed route 20 Halton as a destination, as seen on Feltham car 526 passing through the woods.

With a delightful backdrop of slag heaps from one of the many local collieries, a Horsfield car passes one of the intermediate stops on the Middleton tramway, as folk patiently await their tram in the opposite direction.

Above and below: While the vast majority of the Leeds tram fleet was of double-deck configuration, three experimental single-deckers were obtained. Number 600 (above) had been new to Sunderland Corporation in 1930, but was rebuilt before re-entering service in Leeds in 1954. No. 602 (below) was one of two with thirty-four-seat (plus plenty of standees) bodies built by Charles H. Roe at Crossgates, Leeds, new in 1953. After closure of the system in 1959, both were transported to what is now the National Tramway Museum at Crich. Here, on 6 May 1960, they are seen passing Doncaster Racecourse on their way to their new home, being towed by one of Elliots of York's Scammells. At the time of writing, 600 is in store at Clay Cross, while 602 is usually to be found on static display in the main exhibit building.

A typical Leeds City Transport vehicle of the pre-Second World War period is this 1934-built AEC Regent, with a fifty-six-seat Roe body, fleet number 139 (ANW 682). Fortunately, it has been preserved and was photographed in central Leeds in September 1986. Today, it resides in the Keighley Bus Museum and still sees regular outings. The blue colour scheme seen here later gave way to two-tone green, as illustrated in the next photograph.

Another Roe-bodied AEC seating fifty-six, this time it is a Regent III, delivered in 1950. No. 612 (NUB 612) was photographed in Farsley in March 1968. (Les Flint)

The Roe-bodied AEC Regent III was certainly a popular choice for Leeds City Transport. Here is a 1949 example, No. 466 (MUG 466), seen on a short working on Kirkstall Road, near Kirkstall Valley Primary School.

Leeds continued to order AEC double-deckers into the 1960s. Delivered in 1960 was No. 913 (3913 UB), an AEC Regent V, with Metro-Cammell seventy-one-seat bodywork. It was photographed passing the central bus station in 1973.

With the introduction of the more modern AEC Regent V, Leeds City Transport continued to add these into the fleet. Towards the end of its life, in 1973, No. 980 (ENW 980D) was photographed in the central bus station. Standard Roe seventy-seat bodywork is carried.

A slightly earlier AEC Regent V, built in 1963, No. 940 (940 GUA) is seen in the yard of Bramley depot, *c.* 1974, just before West Yorkshire PTE took over.

Leeds City Transport did not standardise solely on AEC buses bodied by Roe. No. 315 (315 DUA) in the fleet was a 1962 Leyland PD3A/2 with Metro-Cammell H39/31R bodywork. It was photographed passing the open market and the bus station in central Leeds in 1973.

The usual seventy-seat Roe bodywork is carried on this Daimler CVG6LX delivered to Leeds in 1963. This photograph of No. 583 (583 FUM) was taken on the same occasion and from a nearly identical viewpoint as the other on this page.

More bodywork by Roe, this time on a Leyland PD3/5 chassis, built in 1959. No. 272 (5272 NW) is seen at Bramley depot in 1973.

No. 214 (UUA 214) in the Leeds City Transport fleet was given a new lease of life after withdrawal from normal service as it became a driver training vehicle. This 1955-built Leyland PD2/11 with a Roe body is seen on York Street in Leeds in 1973.

Inevitably, Leeds City Transport later purchased rear-engined double-deck buses, such as No. 160 (PUB 160G), a Daimler Fleetline with dual-doored Roe bodywork. It is seen in the bus station, with the parish church looking down on it, in 1973.

The single-deck vehicles of Leeds City Transport rarely frequented the city centre, being mainly confined to the peripheral routes, such as 89 to Horsforth. Operating this service on a winter's day around 1974, just after the PTE took over, is No. 1253 (JNW 953E), captured on film in Pudsey.

Still in full LCT livery, though West Yorkshire PTE legal lettering has appeared, No. 109 (109 LNW) heads along York Street into the city centre. New in 1964, this Daimler Fleetline was fitted with a seventy-seat Roe body.

The changes have begun. At Torre Road depot is a pair of 1960-built AEC Regent V buses, both with Metro-Cammell bodywork. On the left, 917 (3917 UB) carries 'Metro Leeds' identity, while 921 (3921 UB) retains its full LCT paintwork.

In 1970, Leeds City Transport acquired half a dozen Mercedes L405D/Williams Deansgate thirteen-seat minibuses for use on a city centre service. On 3 August 1974, in PTE ownership, No. 34 (YUA 534J) enters the central bus station alongside Leyland Atlantean 501 (JUG 501L).

The first day of April 1974 saw Leeds City Transport become integrated into West Yorkshire Passenger Transport Executive. The same fate befell the other former municipal operators in the county, including Bradford Corporation Transport. Leeds and Bradford had long run a joint route between the two cities. On such a duty, arriving at its Leeds terminus, on 3 August 1974 is former Bradford Corporation No. 428 (PKE 428J), now numbered 2428 in PTE ownership. This dual-doored Alexander-bodied Daimler Fleetline had been new in October 1970.

The new West Yorkshire PTE livery is revealed on No. 110 (110 LNW), a former Leeds City Transport 1964-built Daimler Fleetline with seventy-seat Roe bodywork, photographed in Leeds bus station, *c.* 1977.

With the PTE taking over the former municipal fleets, inevitably there were some inter-depot transfers. Here is a good example. No. 51 (PXO 974) is seen in Leeds some time around 1975, having previously operated in Halifax. This AEC Reliance, originally built in 1955, had been new to Timpson's of London with a centre-entrance Plaxton body. It was later sold to the Halifax Joint Omnibus Committee and rebodied, again by Plaxton, but with a conventional forty-three-seat front-entrance layout.

Another Roe-bodied Daimler Fleetline, No. 209 (JUM 209L), this time with a dual-door layout and seating seventy-eight passengers is seen below Leeds City railway station in the spring of 1980. It had been new to Leeds City Transport as fleet No. 759 in 1972.

The Leeds City Transport colour scheme did not disappear overnight. In 1976, former LCT AEC Regent V No. 971 (DUM 971C) was photographed sandwiched between Leyland Fleetline 7033 (MNW 33P) and Leyland Atlantean AN68A/1R 8092 (LUG 92P), both new to the PTE. All three buses carry Roe bodywork. The location is the depot yard in Call Lane, central Leeds.

Towards the end of its existence Leeds City Transport turned to the AEC Swift for its single-deck requirements. Now in PTE colours and photographed in Leeds in 1979 was No. 1274 (MNW 174F), with unusual MCW forty-eight-seat dual-door bodywork, looking almost American in its appearance.

Number 1070 (AUB 170J) in both the Leeds and PTE fleets and seen in the latter's livery, this AEC Swift carried Roe bodywork, to the same specification as that of 1274 (above). It is seen in central Leeds with a good load of passengers on a private hire.

One of the first single-deck buses to be delivered to West Yorkshire PTE was No. 38 (JUG 354N), seen at Leeds City railway station in 1977. This short, twenty-seven-seat Bristol LHS6L/ECW saloon was one of a small batch purchased in 1975 for a service around central Leeds. They did not last long in Yorkshire, this one later seeing service with Merseyside PTE, Nottingham City Transport and Busways (Newcastle). It was to become a driver training vehicle in 1989.

Delivery of a large batch of Leyland Atlantean AN68/1R double-deckers, bodied by Roe to H43/33F configuration, commenced in 1974. Delivered in December of the year, No. 6039 (GUG 566N) was photographed in Leeds bus station in spring 1981. By that date the MetroBus branding had been adopted.

A typical vehicle in the PTE fleet of the early 1980s, 6277 (PUA 277W), a Roe-bodied Leyland Atlantean AN68C/1R, is seen in Leeds bus station with a Metropolitan double-decker from the Bradford fleet alongside in spring 1981.

In 1980, West Yorkshire PTE received its first batch of just ten MCW MetroBus seventy-seven double-deck buses. One of them, No. 7509 (PUA 509W), is seen here, passing the bus station in early 1981. More MetroBuses were to follow, but were either bodied by Alexander or were of the Mark II version.

Only ten Alexander-bodied MCW MetroBuses were built for West Yorkshire PTE and were delivered in 1982. One of them, No. 7518 (UWW 518X), is seen not long after delivery, in Leeds bus station.

The MCW MetroBus II proved more popular with West Yorkshire PTE and a total of sixty were received between 1982 and 1984. One of these seventy-six-seat MCW-bodied vehicles, No. 7529 (CUB 529Y), was photographed in pristine condition at Torre Road depot not long after delivery.

The first Leyland Olympians appeared in the PTE fleet in 1981, all with bodywork built by Roe. These, totalling over one-hundred, continued to be received until 1984. No. 5049 (CUB 49Y) was new in February 1983 and is seen on a grey spring day in central Leeds the following year.

A small batch of Leyland Tigers with dual-purpose forty-seven-seat Duple Dominant bodies arrived in 1983 and 1984. One of these smart vehicles, No. 1667 (A667 KUM), was photographed passing Leeds Corn Exchange not long after entering service.

With deregulation coming in 1986 and privatisation on the horizon, a rebranding exercise saw the bus operations taking the name Yorkshire Rider, while coaches were identified by Gold Rider lettering. Painted in the new colours and photographed in Leeds on a misty winter's day in early 1987 is No. 1401 (C401 EWU). This Volvo B10M-61 with fifty-three-seat Jonckheere coachwork had been delivered in June 1986.

The mid to late 1980s saw a great outbreak of minibuses on Britain's roads and West Yorkshire was no exception. Branded as Micro Rider, here's a typical example in Leeds bus station in late 1987. No. 1725 (D725 JUB) is a sixteen-seat Freight Rover Sherpa, the coachwork being fitted out by Carlyle.

Another minibus with the Micro Rider name, this time a VW LT55 with twenty-five-seat Optare City Pacer bodywork. No. 2019 (E219 PWY) is seen on Boar Lane, Leeds, with City Square behind, just before Christmas in 1987.

The CB3/5/7 routes from Leeds city centre ran out through Woodlouse and Armley, with the CB3 continuing on to Cottingley. This gave a twenty-minute frequency on the core section of the route, but only hourly on the CB3 itself. Given the limited capacity of the vehicle in use on this service in spring 1987, it does make one wonder if a larger bus would have been more suitable. Nevertheless, No. 1704 (D704 HUA), a Freight Rover Sherpa completed by Optare to become a sixteen-seat minibus, is seen passing the main entrance to City station.

It was not unknown for Yorkshire Rider to acquire second-hand vehicles. The one illustrated here, a Northern Counties-bodied Leyland Fleetline, had been new to Greater Manchester PTE as No. 8045 (ANA 45T). As Yorkshire Rider's Halifax fleet No. 7231, it is seen leaving Leeds bus station on a long journey to Rishworth.

In 1989, Yorkshire Rider completed the purchase of the West Yorkshire Road Car Company. Included in the sale was DWU 298T, given the number 715 in its new guise. This Bristol VRT/SL3/6LXB, built in 1978, was given a new ECW body a year later. It is seen fully dressed for its Leeds operations in the bus station in 1990. It would later be transferred to First Eastern National.

Another acquisition from West Yorkshire Road Car Company, this fifty-two-seat Leyland National saloon, originally numbered 1496, is seen as Yorkshire Rider Leeds 1341 (JUB 647V). It was photographed turning off The Headrow into the heart of the city on a wet autumn day in 1990.

Based in Huddersfield, No. 1454 (G454 JYG) is about to return there as it loads up in Leeds bus station in 1990. Despite the long-distance nature of the route, passengers must endure bus-type seating in the Volvo B10M-55/Plaxton Derwent II saloon.

Yorkshire Rider painted Mark II MCW MetroBus No. 7575 (B575 RWY) into a version of the old Leeds City Transport colours. As such, it is seen in central Leeds in early 1988.

Another double-decker painted into a retro livery, Roe-bodied Leyland Olympian No. 5035 (CUB 35Y) has the colours of the early Leeds trams, as it prepares for departure in Leeds bus station, summer 1989.

In keeping with the traditions of its predecessors, Yorkshire Rider used singe-deck buses on its services that did not penetrate Leeds city centre. Operating Ring Road service 8 in 1991 is No. 1251 (G252 JYG), a DAF SB220 with forty-seven-seat Optare Delta bodywork. It is photographed in Pudsey bus station.

New in 1990, Yorkshire Rider No. 8008 (H808 TWX) takes on passengers in Leeds bus station in the year of manufacture. It was one of just five Northern Counties-bodied Scania N113DRB vehicles, though others of the same chassis design were ordered but bodied by Alexander.

One of the first Scania N113DRB types received by Yorkshire Rider, No. 8004 (G804 JYG), delivered in March 1990, calls at New Market Street, central Leeds, in the autumn of that year. Eighty-seat Alexander bodywork is carried.

Yorkshire Rider's 3001–3006 were Alexander-bodied Volvo B6-50 types, each seating forty passengers. No. 3005 (L105 PWR) of this batch passes the Corn Exchange in autumn 1994.

No. 5516 (D516 HUB), an Optare-bodied Leyland Olympian in the Yorkshire Rider fleet, had received the red livery of the erstwhile West Yorkshire Road Car Company when photographed in Leeds in 1995. When new in 1987, it had been fitted with coach seats.

Another Yorkshire Rider bus in a commemorative colour scheme, on behalf of Leeds Development Corporation. The recipient is MCW MetroBus Mark II No. 7577 (B577 RWY), seen in central Leeds on 5 August 1995. (Richard Huggins)

One of the Scania N113CRB saloons, with Alexander forty-eight-seat bodywork, photographed in Superbus livery in central Leeds in summer 1994. No. 8649 (L649 PWR) had entered service in June of that year.

Now bearing the wording 'Rider Leeds', in mid-1995, No. 3253 (M253 VWW) is passing along New Market Street. The forty-seat Dennis Dart/Alexander combination had only been delivered in March. The General Eliott pub, on the left, survives today.

In 1994, Yorkshire Rider had become part of the Badgerline Group that, in turn, developed into First Bus. By spring 1996, when this photograph was taken, the new livery and '*f*' logo had been applied to much of the fleet. Demonstrating the new colours is 4052 (N452 JUG), a Dennis Lance with Plaxton Verde bodywork seating forty-nine passengers. The location is New Market Street, Leeds.

Looking very smart in its new First Bus colours, despite it being a foul day, MCW MetroBus Mark II No. 7566 (B566 RWY) has arrived in Otley's small bus station, autumn 1997.

Under First Bus ownership, each division of the fleet received an individual livery. That of Calderdale is seen here, applied to No. 5313 (L313 PWR), a Northern Counties-bodied Volvo Olympian. It is seen on The Headrow in Leeds, with Halifax as a destination, in spring 1999.

Having been driven down from Scotland, First Bus Grampian No. 514 (L514 KSA), a Mercedes O405 with Optare bodywork seating forty-nine, is seen acting as a demonstrator for the type on Boar Lane in Leeds in mid-1996. In the event, the Leeds operations did not receive any buses of this type.

As the twenty-first century arrived, so did the First Bus corporate livery, applied only to new, low-floor vehicles to begin with. New in 1999, no. 8141 (V141 ESC), a Scania L94UB with forty-three-seat Wright bodywork, displays its new colours as it passes Leeds Corn Exchange in the spring of 2000.

Looking outwardly similar to 8141 (above), No. 8453 (R453 JFS) has a Scania L113CRL chassis with a Wright body seating just forty passengers. Branded as a Superbus, it is fitted with guide wheels for use on a short section of guided busway. It is about to intersect The Headrow in central Leeds in spring 1999.

Still in its old colours in 1999 is No. 3255 (M255 VWW), a Dennis Dart with Alexander Dash bodywork and forty seats. The location, one of the author's favourite spots, is outside the Corn Exchange in central Leeds.

Now it is November 2004 and First Bus has begun to apply its new livery to older buses and has introduced a five-figure national numbering system. Given the identity of 31118, H641 VNW is seen picking up in New Market Street, Leeds. New in 1991, it is a Scania N113DRB with Alexander bodywork.

As early as 1999, the First Bus colours were becoming common and are seen here applied to this 1998-built Optare Solo, No. 2301 (S301 EWU). Lettered as a Quickstep vehicle (already absorbed into the main Leeds operation), it is seen on Duncan Street in Leeds city centre.

Another Optare Solo with First, No. 53901 (YK55 ENT), a thirty-two-seat vehicle, is loading up on the free city centre service at Leeds City railway station on 11 August 2006. At the time of writing, this area is undergoing major reconstruction.

With the introduction of a nationwide corporate livery, transfers with the First Bus Group became easier. No. 30743 (P195 TGD), an Alexander-bodied Volvo Olympian, had been new in 1996 with Strathclyde Buses. On 11 August 2006, it is seen on New Market Street, Leeds.

In a special colour scheme for Leeds University services is First Bus No. 31763 (R924 WOE), another Volvo Olympian with Alexander bodywork, photographed beside Leeds City station on 16 February 2008. It had been new as a dual-doored bus with Stanwell Buses (Westlink) in London.

The low-floor double-deck bus has now arrived in Leeds. New in 2001, No. 30942 (Y797 XNW), an Alexander-bodied Dennis Trident, is turning into New Market Street, Leeds, on 2 September 2012.

In a striking silver livery, First Bus No. 39221 (BP11 JWA) negotiates City Square in Leeds on 17 July 2014. It is a Volvo B5LH with sixty-four-seat Wright bodywork, one of many similar types to join the fleet.

Ordered for city operations in York, the Volvo B7LA/Wright articulated buses looked very impressive, but did not prove popular. They were soon transferred to West Yorkshire, for use on Leeds to Bradford services. On such a duty is 19005 (YK06 ATX), see ascending The Headrow in Leeds, 17 July 2014.

Very much the standard First Bus West Yorkshire vehicle of the time, No. 32445 (YJ04 FYS) is seen in New Market Street, Leeds, on 25 May 2017. It is a Volvo B7TL with Wright seventy-four-seat bodywork.

Another Volvo B7TL/Wright double-decker in the First Bus fleet, No. 32472 (YJ04 FZY), has had Pulse branding applied, to indicate a high-frequency service. On 25 May 2017, it was photographed in central Leeds on an empty working.

Articulated buses have never proved popular with British operators. An example of the more common ones, First Bus No. 10041 (W124 DWX), a Volvo B7LA/Wright fifty-six-seat bus, is seen in central Leeds on a short run to Beeston on 24 April 2014.

First Bus introduced the Wright StreetLite single-deck bus to the streets of Leeds. Here is No. 47640 (SN15 AEG), a thirty-seven-seat example, which had been transferred from its Swansea area operations. On 28 August 2019 it is seen travelling along Boar Lane, passing Tapped Leeds, a well-known establishment brewing its own beer.

For its double-deck needs, First has settled on the Wright StreetDeck as meeting modern requirements. In use on Park & Ride duties and branded as such, No. 35302 (SN18 XXY) turns off Boar Lane in central Leeds on 28 August 2019.

Just a few hints of red contrast with the smart two-tone green livery of First Bus 35514 (SK68 TRV) in City Square, central Leeds, on 10 January 2019. It is one of many Wright StreetDeck vehicles in the fleet to H45/28F configuration.

The electric bus has now hit the streets of Leeds. First No. 68806 (YD70 CGV) is one of nine delivered in 2020, built by Yutong in China. This thirty-four-seat bus is seen in City Square on 19 July 2021 operating route 5 around the central area of the city.

By the 1960s, the West Yorkshire Road Car Company (WYRCC) was very much a standard British Transport Commission (Tilling) business, with vehicles of mainly Bristol chassis and ECW bodies. No. DBW30 (LWR 416) was no exception, being a KSW6B with low-height bodywork seating fifty-five passengers. Platform doors were fitted when new in 1952. It is seen in Otley bus station in October 1967 with a Ledgard's bus behind. (Les Flint)

In Leeds city centre, WYRCC had its own bus station at Vicar Lane. It was a small, rather cramped affair, but it was very convenient for the shops. Seen squeezed between two Bristol RE types is No. 1095 (7908 WY), a 1962-built Bristol MW5G with an ECW dual-purpose body. This photograph was taken sometime around 1973.

WYRCC's red National Bus Company livery was always kept in a clean condition, as demonstrated by No. 1368 (RWR 641K) seen at Vicar Lane in 1980. This Bristol RELL6G/ECW B53F bus had been new to the company in July 1972.

Another Bristol RELL6G, this time with fifty-seat dual-purpose bodywork by ECW, is seen here outside Vicar Lane bus station in 1980. No. 1340 (HWU 662J) had been delivered in 1971 and, under the old scheme, been given the number SRG140.

In common with virtually all NBC subsidiaries, West Yorkshire Road Car received plenty of Bristol VR-type double-deckers, such as No. 1725 (JWT 758V). This VRT/SL3/6LXB was fitted with an ECW body seating seventy-four passengers and is seen when around a year old, in 1980, at Vicar Lane, Leeds.

Nearly all NBC businesses received batches of Leyland National saloons and WRCC was no exception. No. 1441 (GUG 120N), a fifty-two-seat example, was new in 1974 and photographed at Vicar Lane in 1980.

WYRCC had a good number of express services, running to places on the Yorkshire coast such as Bridlington and Scarborough. Purchased for such duties were some Plaxton-bodied forty-nine-seat Leyland Leopard coaches, painted into NBC dual-purpose colours. One of them, No. 2576 (KUB 550V), is seen at its Vicar Lane terminus in 1980.

By the early 1980s, WYRCC's Bristol RELH6G/ECW coaches were looking rather dated, so some received rebuilt front ends, the work being done by Willowbrook. This example, No. 2517 (YYG 540G) of 1969 vintage, looks rather futuristic at Vicar Lane in 1980.

In the 1980s, West Yorkshire PTE livery began to be applied to other companies' vehicles, including those of WYRCC. No. 1453 (GUG 132N), a fifty-two-seat Leyland National, is seen in Otley bus station on a freezing day early in 1986.

With impending privatisation on the horizon, WYRCC became free to introduce a new colour scheme, which looked rather splendid on No. 1815 (FUM 490Y). This ECW-bodied Leyland Olympian is seen reversing out of Vicar Lane bus station, Leeds, heading for Wetherby in early 1988.

In 1967, WYRCC completed the purchase of the business of the Executors of Samuel Ledgard Ltd, who operated a network of services around Otley, Leeds and Bradford. The Ledgard fleet consisted mainly of second-hand buses. A fine example, registered HGF 908, is seen here in Otley bus station, *c.* 1960. It is a former London Transport Daimler CWA6/Park Royal vehicle built in 1946.

CDK 401 in the Ledgard fleet was a 1948 AEC Regent III/East Lancs double-decker, new to Rochdale Corporation. It is seen here towards the end of its life with Ledgard's, in October 1967, at Otley bus station. (Les Flint)

WYRCC was sold to the AJS Group in 1987, with the operations being split up into smaller entities. The Leeds and Bradford part of the business was then passed on to Yorkshire Rider in 1989. West Yorkshire was retained as a fleet name for a short while and is seen applied to No. 6433 (KPJ 291W), a former London Country Leyland Atlantean AN68B/1R with Roe bodywork (to a Park Royal design). It was photographed at Vicar Lane bus station in January 1990, the year that it closed and all services diverted to the Central bus station.

When WYRCC was split up, the Keighley & District operations adopted a rather dull grey and red colour scheme, seen applied to Leyland National 2 No. 287 (UWY 67X). The location is Leeds Central bus station and the date is early in 1991.

One of the first vehicles new to Keighley & District was No. 201 (G293 KWY), a forty-nine-seat Leyland Lynx. It is seen, in early 1990, in Rodley, to the northwest of Leeds, an area once served by Leeds City Tramways.

A much brighter colour scheme has been applied to Keighley & District No. 901 (L648 MYG), a Leyland Olympian with Alexander bodywork. Fitted with bus-type seating, the vehicle was dedicated to route 760, Keighley–Leeds–Wetherby. It was photographed as it entered Leeds bus station in early 1994.

Yorkshire Coastliner was formed out of the longer-distance operations of the Blazefield empire, running from Leeds towards York and the coastal resorts. In early 1995, No. 411 (G112 VMM) is waiting time in Leeds bus station prior to setting out for Whitby via Thornton Dale. This vehicle, a Wadham Stringer-bodied Leyland Swift, had been new to Hertfordshire operator Lucketts of Watford.

Only a few months old when photographed in Leeds in early 1994, Yorkshire Coastliner No. 408 (L8 YCL) looks to be in pristine condition. This Volvo Olympian was the first bus to receive an Alexander Royale body, with seventy-four coach seats. After withdrawal, this vehicle was sold, along with its valuable registration, to Geldards Coaches, based in Leeds.

The West Riding Automobile Company was one of the larger operators running into Leeds; indeed the company was Britain's largest independent until absorbed into the National Bus Company in 1969. The fleet at that time consisted of a great variety of buses, but an unusual one to enter into West Riding ownership was 828 BWY. This forty-five-seat Bristol MW6G/ECW had been new to the West Yorkshire Road Car Co. as number SMG20. Here it is, *c.* 1974, with West Riding as No. 102, with a standard Bristol RE saloon behind at the central bus station in Leeds.

When the NBC took over West Riding it inherited a large batch of Guy Wulfrunians, which, understandably, soon went for disposal. As a temporary replacement, more conventional double-deckers were transferred in from other NBC constituents. One of them, No. 542 (HHY 181D), was photographed in Leeds, *c.* 1974. This ECW-bodied Bristol FLF6G had been new to the Bristol Omnibus Company.

Still in service in 1977 was this West Riding Leyland Panther with Roe fifty-one-seat bodywork, photographed in the central bus station in Leeds. When new it carried the fleet No. 140, but was later renamed 241 (JHL 140E).

Another fifty-one-seat Leyland Panther in the West Riding fleet, No. 231 (LHL 175F), this time bodied by Marshall. Again, the location is the central bus station in Leeds. It would be fair to say that the Leyland Panther did not find favour within the NBC fleets and all became early withdrawal candidates.

Takeover by the National Bus Company saw West Riding receive some more standard vehicles, such as this Bristol VRT/SL3/6LX with seventy-four-seat ECW bodywork. No. 757 (OWW 903P), when almost new, in Leeds bus station.

In 1976 West Riding purchased a batch of just five Leyland Leopards with Plaxton dual-purpose forty-nine-seat bodies, though similar ones had been acquired earlier. No. 326 (AHL 726K) loads up for Garforth not long after being delivered.

Under NBC management, vehicles from West Riding and Yorkshire Woollen used on express services carried both fleet names. Here they are applied to No. 379 (HWY 719N), one of a batch of eleven Leyland Leopard/Alexander Y-type forty-nine-seat dual-purpose saloons delivered in 1975. It would have been almost new when photographed entering Leeds bus station on service X5.

Also with dual fleet names, plus MetroBus branding, No. 562 (A562 KWY) basks in the sun in late 1984 at Leeds bus station. This Leyland Olympian had ECW bodywork fitted out with seventy comfortable coach seats.

Under Caldaire ownership, West Riding adopted a new green and cream livery, as seen on Leyland National No. 143 (PWW 717R). It was photographed in 1987 heading out of Leeds, through City Square and bound for Knottingley.

In a version of MetroBus livery, branded for Fastaway services, West Riding No. 616 (C616 ANW), a Leyland Olympian with coach-seated ECW bodywork, is captured on film in City Square, Leeds, in the spring of 1967. Its destination, on route X13, is Grimethorpe, near Barnsley.

The Leyland Lynx was to feature heavily in the West Riding fleets in Caldaire days. Most were bought new, but this one, No. 253 (D204 FBK), had been new to an independent called Hants & Sussex. Wearing advertising livery, it is seen in Leeds in autumn 1990.

Selby & District was a branding exercise applied to West Riding buses based in that town. Photographed in Leeds bus station in 1993, heading for York via Selby, is No. 405 (K405 HWX). It is a Volvo B10B-58 with fifty-one-seat Alexander Strider bodywork.

The two versions of Caldaire Group's Yorkshire fleets are illustrated here, in New Market Street, Leeds, in December 1991. Closest to the camera, in Yorkshire Woollen District red and cream is Leyland Lynx 2 No. 367 (J367 YWX), almost new at the time.

In all-over NBC red, at Leeds bus station in spring 1981, is Yorkshire Woollen District No. 12 (PUM 675P), one of just four Leyland National fifty-two-seat buses to arrive in 1976.

With its NBC red livery split by a broad white band, Yorkshire Woollen District No. 700 (LHD 310K) is seen having a rest in the parking area of Leeds bus station. One of many Daimler Fleetlines to enter the fleet, this one has ECW bodywork seating seventy-four passengers.

The Yorkshire Woollen fleet later saw Leyland Atlanteans meet its double-deck requirement, such as No. 772 (MUS 869P). Painted in advertising livery for National Holidays, this AN68/1R with Park Royal bodywork was photographed in Leeds bus station in the spring of 1981.

With privatisation, Yorkshire Woollen District became part of the Caldaire Group and a simple red and white livery was introduced, with Yorkshire Buses as a fleet name. Wearing its new colours is Leyland National 2 No. 235 (NAT 202V). It had been new to East Yorkshire Motor Services and is seen arriving at Leeds bus station in autumn 1990.

Yorkshire Woollen's PUB 68W, a Willowbrook coach-seated Leyland Leopard, had been delivered to West Riding as No. 68 in 1981. Here it is in early 1988, having been renumbered as 22, at Leeds bus station, lettered for express 'Fastaway' services.

Another vehicle in Yorkshire Buses livery, No. 42 (C42 CWT) stands awaiting duty in Leeds bus station in March 1991. This Leyland Tiger with forty-nine-seat Plaxton Paramount coachwork had been delivered to the West Riding Group in January 1986.

Resplendent in the last Yorkshire Buses colour scheme is No. 809 (L809 NNW), a Dennis Lance with Alexander Strider bodywork seating forty-nine passengers. The photograph was taken outside Leeds Corn Exchange in 1994.

The operations of both West Riding and Yorkshire Woollen District became part of Arriva in the late 1990s and vehicles soon began to appear in the new corporate livery. Unlike Stagecoach and First Bus, no group-wide fleet numbering system was adopted, so M817 RCP was numbered 27. It is seen here leaving Duncan Street in central Leeds in the spring of 2000. This DAF SB220, with Ikarus bodywork, had been acquired from K-Line of Huddersfield.

One of many Leyland Lynx saloons from the Yorkshire Woollen and West Riding fleets, No. 277 (F277 AWW), a forty-nine-seat example, had been new to the former. Here it is in Arriva colours passing the Corn Exchange in Leeds in spring 1999.

Low-floor buses were soon introduced to the Arriva Yorkshire fleet. A double-deck example, No. 656 (W656 CWX), a seventy-five-seat Volvo B7TL with Alexander bodywork, was photographed in Duncan Street, Leeds, in early 2000.

Some of Arriva's principal routes were given 'Max' status with buses branded accordingly. These included the 202 and 203 Leeds to Huddersfield services. On 25 May 2017, Alexander Dennis E40D/Alexander H45/31F No. 1918 (SN15 LLG) is about to leave Leeds city centre as it passes the Corn Exchange.

Yorkshire Traction's buses were frequent visitors to Leeds bus station. Having arrived on an X32 service from Sheffield, No. 673 (C673 GET) is having a rest prior to loading up and returning in summer 1991. When new, this ECW-bodied Leyland Olympian had been fitted with bus seats, but was later given coach seating for express duties.

No. 332 (F702 CWJ) in the Yorkshire Traction fleet, a twenty-three-seat MCW Metrorider, had been new to Sheffield operator SUT. In Yorkshire Traction's hands it had passed to their Huddersfield depot and was found in Leeds bus station in early 1992.

In December 2005 Yorkshire Traction was sold to the Stagecoach Group. Three years later, the Huddersfield operations were passed on to Centrebus Holdings and then to Arriva Yorkshire, but operating under the name of Yorkshire Tiger. Seen in City Square, Leeds, in the new orange colours is No. 775 (YJ10 EZH), a thirty-eight-seat Optare Tempo saloon.

Yorkshire Tiger No. 893 (V313 GLB) is a Dennis Trident with Alexander bodywork that had been new to Metroline for its London operations. It is seen on Boar Lane, Leeds, on 24 April 2014 nearing journey's end at the bus station. In 2021 Yorkshire Tiger was sold to Transdev and now operates under the title of Team Pennine.

The vehicles of East Yorkshire Motor Services were often to be found in Leeds on express duties. Heading for Bridlington in 1975 is No. 772 (9772 RH), a 1964-built Leyland Leopard with dual-purpose Willowbrook coachwork. Still in its pre-NBC blue, it was photographed in Wellington Street coach station, Leeds.

After the closure of Wellington Street, East Yorkshire transferred their express services to Vicar Lane bus station. It is here, around 1981, that we see No. 921 (BKH 921K), a Plaxton-bodied Leyland Leopard forty-nine-seat coach in National Express white.

For a short while in the later years of the 1980s, Potteries Motor Traction (PMT) began operations in and around Leeds. Many miles away from its Staffordshire heartland, fleet No. 528 (E528 JRE) was photographed on service in Pudsey in late 1987. This Rootes Group Dodge S56/Alexander twenty-five-seat minibus was almost brand new at the time.

A larger PMT vehicle, Bristol VRT/SL3/501 No. 715 (GRF 715V), with ECW bodywork, is seen resting in the Central bus station in Leeds in early in 1988. PMT's West Yorkshire operations did not last long.

Lancaster City Transport introduced route 200 in the early 1990s, running from Leeds to Morecambe via Ingleton. On a cold day in January 1992 there are unlikely to be hordes of passengers wishing to travel to the coast, but local passengers could also be carried. Waiting for its next duty in Leeds is 644 (WAO 644Y), an ex-Cumberland Motor Services Leyland Tiger with Alexander coach-seated bodywork.

Lancaster City Transport sold out to the Stagecoach Group in 1993, who continued the service for a while, even extending it to Doncaster. With Ribble fleet names and branded as the Lancashire Coastliner, Dennis Javelin/Plaxton forty-seven-seat coach No. 139 (L139 BFV) was photographed in Leeds bus station in the summer of 1994.

After the sale of West Riding Automobile Services to the British Transport Commission, Leeds-based Wallace Arnold became the largest independent in the UK. The company's main business was touring and their coaches could be seen throughout Europe. At the yard on The Calls in Leeds in 1980, as a High Speed Train passes, are SWW 141R and XWX 190S, both being Duple-bodied Leyland Leopards.

Wallace Arnold also undertook a small amount of stage carriage work in the Leeds area, using the names of companies taken over: Farsley Omnibus and Kippax & District. In the livery of the latter, at Leeds bus station in March 1968, is 6237 UB, a Roe-bodied Leyland PD3/1 delivered new in 1960. Wallace Arnold's Leeds area bus routes were sold to Leeds City Transport later in 1968. (Les Flint)

The suburb of Horsforth was always worth a visit in the late 1970s, to look at the vehicles of Independent Coachways. The company used a variety of double-deck buses on schools and contract duties. One of the more unusual ones was VYH 47G, a Roe-bodied Leyland Atlantean PDR2/1 that had been new to Hall's of Hounslow and used on British Airways contracts to London Heathrow Airport. It is seen in the company's yard in 1978.

GCN 2N in the Independent Coachways fleet was one of only three Volvo Ailsa B55-10 buses that had been new to Tyne & Wear PTE. All were bodied by Alexander. This one looks splendid in the green livery at its new home in 1979. GCN 2N was later to enter preservation.

Pontefract-based South Yorkshire Road Transport ran a couple of services between Leeds and Doncaster. Arriving at the central bus station in Leeds on 3 August 1974 is one of many double-deck vehicles in the fleet, No. 90 (HWR 690J), a 1971-built Leyland Atlantean PDR1/3 with seventy-seat Northern Counties bodywork.

Preparing for its long run to Doncaster is South Yorkshire Road Transport No. 106 (H106 RWT), seen loading up in Leeds in 1990. Almost new at the time, this Northern Counties-bodied Leyland Olympian would prove to be one of the last double-deck buses ordered by this company, as South Yorkshire Road Transport fell into the hands of the Caldaire Group in 1994.

Black Prince was probably the best known of the post-deregulation independents that sprang into life in the Leeds area. Operating mainly on the Leeds to Morley corridor, the smart livery soon became familiar to Leonians. The company developed a liking for the front-engined Volvo B55-10 Ailsa marque. One of many purchased was KSD 94W, an Alexander-bodied example, new to Western Scottish. It was photographed passing the Corn Exchange in central Leeds in early 1994.

A more unusual Ailsa in the Black Prince fleet was LWB 377P, bodied in Ireland by Van Hool McArdle. New to South Yorkshire PTE, it retained its dual-door layout with Black Prince and received a special green colour scheme commemorating the company's silver jubilee. It is seen in Vicar Lane, Leeds, in September 1994.

Black Prince also purchased several single-deck buses and a good example is 213 (213 ONU). This Leyland National Greenway forty-nine-seat saloon had been converted in 1993 by East Lancashire Coachbuilders from Leyland National SKG 924S that had been new to Western Welsh. The location is New Market Street, Leeds, in early 1994.

Black Prince later purchased a good number of Scania buses. One of them was RUH 15Y, a BR112DH type, with forty-two-seat Wadham Stringer bodywork. It had started life in the fleet of Newport Transport, South Wales. This photograph was taken in spring 1999, again on New Market Street.

Another ex-Newport Scania in the Black Prince fleet, No. 100 (PTG 100Y), a BR112DH-type double-decker bodied by Marshall, photographed on The Headrow, central Leeds, in May 1999.

Not all the vehicles in the Black Prince fleet were second-hand. S902 DUB, given the fleet number 902, was a Mercedes O405 with Optare Prisma forty-nine-seat bodywork. It is seen in central Leeds in May 1999. Black Prince succumbed to the might of the First Group in 2005.

Whether the Quickstep operations were independent is debateable, but outwardly they seemed to be. One of the minibuses used in Leeds was E463 TYG, a nineteen-seat Iveco 49.10 bodied by Robin Hood. It is seen laying over in Leeds bus station in spring 1994.

Quickstep soon became absorbed into the main First Bus fleet, but the identity remained until at least autumn 1997, when this photograph was taken in central Leeds. Bearing Quickstep Travel decals on its First livery is No. 2258 (M258 VWU), a Plaxton-bodied Mercedes 709D twenty-seat minibus.

Ivy Coaches mainly ran services around Dewsbury and Huddersfield, but their vehicles also found their way into Leeds. Departing from Leeds bus station, heading for Huddersfield on route 20, in late 1987 is PFM 869M, a former Crosville Leyland National with dual-purpose seating.

Stanley Gath Travel mainly operated schools and contract services, but one of their buses was found in central Leeds in autumn 1990. Still in all-over red, Leyland National THX212S retained its dual-doored layout from its previous owner, London Buses.

Rhodes Coaches took up operation of several routes in the Leeds area after deregulation, with a base at Yeadon. It is here, in spring 1989, that we see DKH 931L, a former East Yorkshire Motor Services Bristol VRT/SL6G with seventy-seat ECW bodywork.

A more unusual bus in the Rhodes fleet was A105 FPL, a coach-seated Leyland Olympian that had been new as LRC5 in the London Country fleet and used on Green Line services. Here it is in central Leeds on a more mundane duty, heading out to Whinmoor in the city's eastern suburbs. This photograph was taken in the summer of 1993, not long before Rhodes ceased operating stage carriage services.

Taylors Coaches was another independent that took advantages of deregulation to commence bus operation in Leeds. Seen passing the Corn Exchange in early 1993 is MRB 804P, a Bristol VRT/SL3/6LX bodied by ECW that had been new to Midland General (Trent Motor Traction).

Taylors was later taken over by the K-Line organisation, which mainly operated in the Huddersfield area. Seen in its new colours, but still carrying Taylors identity, M815 RCP was photographed in New York Street, Leeds, in mid-1995. This forty-nine-seat Ikarus-bodied DAF SB220 had been new to K-Line in October of the previous year.

Black Prince was not the only independent to purchase Volvo Ailsa types for its stage service. Four Seasons, operating out to the east of the city, had JOV 775P, a former West Midlands PTE example bodied by Alexander. It is seen on Boar Lane in late 1991.

Optional Bus was a short-lived entity using a smart colour scheme, as demonstrated by PCA 423V. This Bristol VRT/SL3/501 with ECW bodywork had been new to Crosville, where it bore the fleet number DVL423. It is seen descending The Headrow in central Leeds in spring 1999.

Connexions Buses, a company mainly operating in the Harrogate area, has now gained some operations in West Yorkshire, including Leeds itself. This photograph, taken on 6 September 2012, shows N253 BKK leaving Otley bus station. A forty-three-seat Wright-bodied Scania L113CRL, it had been new to Kentish Bus in 1995.

Also seen in Otley, in June 2004, is Y2 UTO, a sixteen-seat Mercedes 614D belonging to a local firm called Utopia who had gained the contract to operate route 923 to Wetherby. The contract for this service has since passed to Connexions Buses.

Amberley Coaches was another operator that took to stage carriage work after deregulation. Many vehicles operated in the colours of their previous owners, but Leyland National KCG 608L wore the company's livery as it arrived in the bus station in Leeds in early 1988. Fifteen years earlier, the bus had been new to Alder Valley.

Geldard's Coaches, trading as Bigfoot Buses, ran a bit of stage carriage work in the mid-1990s. A black and yellow livery was employed, as seen on CFM 357S, photographed in central Leeds in December 1995. This Leyland National had been new to Crosville, numbered SML357, in 1978.

SUT was a Sheffield-based company operating out of a depot in that city that had previously been used by National Express. A local service, route 90, was being operated in Leeds in the summer of 1988 and RMA 315P was photographed on that duty in the central bus station. This Plaxton-bodied Leyland Leopard coach had been new to Crosville as fleet number CLL315.

Some of the buses used on route 90 received Airebus names and colours. One of those vehicles was MLK 672L, a former London Buses Daimler Fleetline/Park Royal, new as DMS672. It is seen in Leeds Central bus station in December 1987.

Fourway, a Leeds-based coach operator, gained a contract to operate route 30 from Pudsey to Horsforth. Seen near the latter terminus is YY64 GTF, a twenty-nine-seat Alexander Dennis Enviro E20D, photographed on 16 January 2015.

Another small independent is SquarePeg, who run service number 31, a Horsforth local. Operating this on 27 July 2023 was another Alexander Dennis Enviro, SN08 AAU, which had been new to National Express. SquarePeg also serves the Seacroft area of Leeds. (Andrew Stopford)

AJC Coaches (also trading as Angloblue) was a small operator based near the Leeds United football ground at Elland Road. Seen here in autumn 1991 is NTT 319M which had been acquired from another Leeds independent, Amberley Coaches. This Marshall-bodied Bristol LH6L coach was new to Western National.

In addition to coaching duties, AJC undertook a small amount of stage carriage work in Leeds. Operating service 68 is XEU 858T, a former Bristol Omnibus Company Leyland National originally delivered with forty-four seats. It was photographed on The Headrow in central Leeds in autumn 1994.

Another small operator that gained a foothold on stage carriage work in Leeds was AB Cars. TTV 754X, a Dodge S56/Reeve Burgess minibus, is seen entering City Square on route 161 to Swillington in autumn 1990. This vehicle had been new to the East Midlands Area of the National Coal Board.

A most unusual bus was employed by a firm called Aztecbird on services from Leeds to the airport and Otley. It is at the latter location that we see Neoplan forty-five-seat saloon V95 EAK in 2002. It was one of a pair built for Hallmark of Luton. (Richard Simons)

For only a short while, Pride of the Road, a Barnsley area independent, ran services in Leeds. In early 1991, Leyland National PTF 729L was photographed in Leeds bus station. It had been new to Ribble Motor Services as a dual-doored vehicle in 1972.

Only a few months old when photographed in Leeds in early 1991, H220 TCP in the Pride of the Road fleet was clearly intended to be a demonstrator. This DAF SB220 had Ikarus bodywork seating fifty passengers when new. Pride of the Road passed into the hands of the Yorkshire Traction Group in 1992.

No book about buses around Leeds would be complete without taking a look at the factory producing bodywork for many vehicles of Leeds City Transport and plenty of other operators. Founded in 1917, Charles H. Roe set up his factory in the eastern suburbs of the city, at Cross Gates. Seen outside the works, brand new in 1933, is Doncaster Corporation No. 43 (DT 4148), a Dennis Lancet with thirty-two-seat bodywork.

A product of the Cross Gates factory, registered SWT 644, has returned to the Roe factory with a group of enthusiasts from Doncaster, *c.* 1962. Belonging to Premier Coaches (Wilson) of Stainforth, near Doncaster, this bus is a Guy Arab IV with bodywork seating sixty-five passengers. The Roe business later became part of British Leyland, closing in 1984 but reopening a year later as Optare. That company is still trading today, but has moved to Sherburn-in-Elmet. The name Charles Henry Roe continues on in Cross Gates, as the local Wetherspoons pub.